Watercolor Sketching

Watercolor Sketching

AN INTRODUCTION

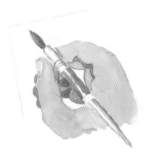

PAUL LASEAU

W·W· NORTON & COMPANY · NEW YORK · LONDON

For information about permission to reproduce selections from
this book, write to Permissions, W. W. Norton & Company, Inc.,
500 Fifth Avenue, New York, NY 10110

For information about special discounts for bulk purchases,
please contact W. W. Norton Special Sales at
specialsales@wwnorton.com or 800-233-4830

Manufacturing by KHL Printing Co.Pte Ltd
Book design by Toni Krass
Electronic production: Joe Lops
Production manager: Leeann Graham

Library of Congress Cataloging-in-Publication Data

Laseau, Paul, 1937–
Watercolor sketching : an introduction / Paul Laseau. — 1st ed.
    p. cm.
Includes bibliographical references and index.
ISBN 978-0-393-73348-8 (pbk.)
1. Watercolor painting—Technique. I. Title.
ND2420.L37 2012
751.42'2—dc23

                                        2011044966

ISBN: 978-0-393-73348-8 (pbk.)

W. W. Norton & Company, Inc.,
500 Fifth Avenue, New York, N.Y. 10110
www.wwnorton.com

W. W. Norton & Company Ltd.,
Castle House, 75/76 Wells Street, London W1T 3QT

0 9 8 7 6 5 4 3 2 1

CREDITS

Unless noted otherwise, all illustrations
and photos are by the author.

CONTENTS

Afternoon Haze by Charles Albanese, FAIA

INTRODUCTION

The most important weapon we humans have is between our ears—provided it's loaded.
—Alan Kay

This book about watercolor is specifically concerned with sketching as a means to experience and understand the worlds of environment and ideas. Like the companion book, *Freehand Sketching*, *Watercolor Sketching* introduces this medium as an instrument for stimulation and growth of creativity for designers.

In the early decades of architectural education in the United States, watercolor media played an important role in architectural presentation and study-abroad sketching or documentation. Then, with the advent and broad availability of color photography, less emphasis was placed on watercolor skills. In recent years digital media and developing communication technologies brought new tools to research and design, but the need for training in human communication remains vital so, once again, watercolor media are attracting interest both in education and in practice. Clients and designers are ever more aware of the nuances of the architectural experience and watercolor is the perfect way to communicate such nuances.

Because appropriate design solutions must be based on extensive knowledge of the design possibilities, continuing education and research are critical parts of architectural careers. Watercolor sketching provides an additional tool for investigating and understanding existing and potential solutions to problems of our physical environment. It is no longer a question of what can be built but the quality of what is built.

Appropriate design solutions also depend upon a productive dialogue among designers and the clients and users of environments. Such dialogues are greatly enhanced by the ability to communicate well both visually and verbally in a compelling, personal way.

This book is a resource for both beginners and those returning to watercolor, including traveling architects, artists, and designers setting out to discover the world around them. The intention is to provide a basic guide to the development of watercolor sketching skills and a means of enriching the early design studio experience. For individuals at any stage in their education or career, this book also offers suggestions for more effective graphic communication.

APPROACH

Writers and musicians know well the importance of extensive reading for successful writing or extensive listening for musical composition. Likewise, visual artists—painters, sculptors, and architects—understand that successful artistic creativity depends upon extensive visual exposure.

The exercises and examples throughout this book are bound together by an emphasis on sketching as a means to visual literacy. Drawing affects the way we see and the way we see is an important factor in the effectiveness and quality of our drawings. Similarly, what we see critically affects the way we think. This relationship between sight and thought provides each of us with unique ways to draw and think creatively. That is why it is essential to view seeing and thinking as integral parts of sketching. Line drawings in ink or pencil provide a foundation for recording or creating imagery, but watercolor sketching reaches into the full experience of environment, even surpassing photographs. I encourage you to go beyond the subjects covered here, to immerse yourself in the art of sketching. Just as exercises in composition and perspective are mutually reinforcing, the drawing of people and structures or trees and machinery brings new perceptions and increased sensitivity to each subject.

For some, the prime reason to take up watercolor is to produce paintings that provide a sense of accomplishment. Although such motivation is important, concern about results not only inhibits learning but also hides an even greater source of motivation: the wealth of other experiences that sketching brings.

If you look carefully at the subjects you sketch, a new, exciting world of awareness and delight opens to you. For example, sketching a front porch may reveal the range of considerations hiding in a simple structure:

- the language of a construction system

- the play of light and shadow

- architecture as an expression of self

- the transition from personal to public scale

SKETCHING-SEEING-SKETCHING

Sketching on a regular basis requires you to pay close attention to the visual world around you. With practice, you begin to see things you never noticed before. The illustrations on this page are details of larger sketches, some of which appear elsewhere in this book. In each instance, sketching required a close look at the subject, resulting in a new awareness—the structure of a lighthouse, the configuration of a specific type of tree, the variations in rowboat shapes, turret details, porch framing, the structural support of a traditional windmill mast.

Because sketching hones your ability to "see" and seeing is essential to effective sketching, it is difficult to learn to see before beginning to sketch, and vice versa. So, where do we start? The sketching/seeing dynamic is like a motor that needs a jump start. Motivation is the key—when you derive initial interest or enjoyment from your first sketching efforts, you then begin to see, leading to an improvement in your sketches and increased motivation.

This book provides the necessary tools for you to begin sketching with a basic level of confidence. Your success in learning to sketch fluidly and competently depends heavily on how much you practice. You must be committed to frequent watercolor sketching throughout your career. A positive attitude toward sketching makes practice a pleasure, rather than a task.

To fully reap the benefits that sketching can afford you, keep these guidelines in mind:

- Sketch only what truly interests you.

- Focus on the opportunities, not on the constraints. Don't let time limits, uncomfortable circumstances, or a complex subject cause you stress. Determine what you can reasonably accomplish while still maintaining your satisfaction with the final product.

- Please yourself, not others. Success in watercolor sketching is a highly personal process. It must first work for you if it is ever to be useful to others.

The chapters in this book are arranged so that you can build skills at a reasonable pace. Beginners should start with the first chapter, but more advanced sketchers may start at later chapters that best meet their needs. Chapter one concentrates on immersing the reader in the act of watercolor sketching to develop basic hand-eye coordination and learn the process of "building" sketches. Chapters two and three extend sketch "building" to environmental-scale subjects found in architecture and landscape design, and elaborate on the techniques of sketch construction, tone, and detail rendering. Chapter four offers direction for sketching a variety of environments in the field. Finally, chapter five discusses some of the possibilities for extending the application of watercolor sketching through studio-based methods, including mixed media and digital editing of images.

Watering Cans by Tony Conner

1. BASIC TOOLS AND SKILLS

This chapter introduces you to watercolor by exploring the basic tools and techniques of the media and the hand-eye coordination required to build observation and notation skills. The exercises are designed to familiarize you with the fundamental steps for producing a sketch in watercolor. The chapter is designed to be helpful to both beginners in sketching and those with some experience in either sketching or watercolor.

I started in watercolor after many years of sketching with pen or pencil. Sketching helped me to develop my skills of observation and recording, and I recommend that you try it as preparation for or in conjunction with watercolor. But don't feel intimidated if this is your first introduction to sketching in general. Watercolor has the unique capability of producing the complete range of qualities of the visible world simply and quickly. As with any other skill, watercolor sketching ability or proficiency is the result of continual attempts to replicate what you observe. This means that watercolor sketching must first be enjoyable. My hope is that after completing this book, you'll have an appreciation for the wonderful possibilities of watercolor and the confidence to dive in and enjoy the medium.

EQUIPMENT

You can complete most of the exercises in this book with a basic set of portable equipment. Portability and convenience are essential if you are to keep the habit of sketching. Avoid the temptation to overload yourself with multiple brushes, large color palettes, easels, or other items that are likely to require several minutes of setup time. You want to be able to respond to the motivation of an interesting subject immediately.

It is important, though, that you use quality materials so that watercolor media can respond as it is intended. My equipment includes a seven-by-ten-inch watercolor block (Arches or Fabriano, nine-by-twelve-inch block optional) and a small spiral-bound watercolor sketchpad. I prefer Kolinsky brushes or Kolinsky-synthetic blends, but there are some quality synthetic brands as well. A good brush holds its shape when wet. (I usually travel with a half-inch wash brush, a no. 8 and no.1 or no. 2 round brush, and a fine liner brush.) You also need a portable, closable palette with mixing area and accommodation for at least eight colors. You can buy palettes with color blocks or empty palettes to which you add colors from tubes. You can purchase quality materials from a local art supply shop or order them online from several sites including Blick, Utrecht, Cheap Joe's Art Stuff, and Jerry's Artarama.

Cadmium Yellow	Yellow Ochre	Burnt Umber	Cobalt Blue	Alizarin Crimson	Sap Green	Ultramarine Blue	Cadmium Red
CY / CB	YO / CB	BU / CB	CB / AC	AC / CY	SG / CY	UB / BU	CR / YO
CY / AC	YO / AC	BU / AC	CB / YO	AC / CB	SG / CB	UB / BU (variation)	CR / UB

PAINT

The first step in getting comfortable with water-color is to experience its four basic elements—paint, brushes, paper, and water. A basic set of watercolor paints consists of cadmium yellow, yellow ocher, burnt umber, cobalt blue, and alizarin crimson. With these pigments you can create a full range of color. You may supplement these colors with three additional hues—sap green, ultramarine blue, and cadmium red, for example. It is important to experiment with mixing these colors to discover a range of possibilities and become familiar with some of the combinations. Try mixing up a few swatches such as those shown here. You should begin to experience the changes in color depending on the proportion used of each base color and the amount of water used.

Cold Press

Hot Press

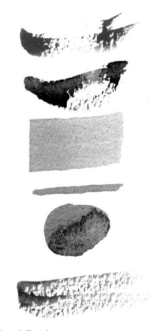

Rough Finish

PAPER

There are three basic types of paper commonly used for watercolor:

- cold press—a slightly textured paper recommended for starting because it's rather forgiving.

- hot press—a very smooth paper that allows colors to float on it, producing a more luminous quality to color.

- rough finish—paper useful for creating textured finishes.

Experiment with each type of paper to fully understand how watercolor behaves on different surfaces.

BRUSHES

Get acquainted with the capabilities and possibilities of your brushes by interacting with water and color applied to a paper surface. Using your sketchpad try the variety of strokes pictured here and combine them in interesting patterns. In doing this, try to be free and spontaneous; you want to experience the many qualities and variations of the media. Vary the intensity of a single color by adding different amounts of water, and then combine colors freely to experience different color effects.

WASHES

As you'll see in later exercises, large areas of colors are often the major organizers of water-color sketches. They are applied at the beginning of the sketch to set the foundation upon which the rest of the sketch is built. The washes used to create these large areas of color vary depending on their role in the sketch. Skies, for example, may be a single color created by a uniform wash throughout the area. They may be a graded wash detecting a change in the color of the sky from near above descending to the horizon, or a varied wash due to cloud formations. To practice, draw squares approximately two inches on a side, and use a wash brush to create a range of washes. Once you feel you have some control over the graded or varied wash, experiment with more complex shapes representing clouds or other atmospheric conditions included in exercises in other chapters of this book. Avoid using too much pigment for the amount of water—this often ignores the transparency of watercolor, creating a rather dull, pasty look (see the examples at the bottom of this page).

Next try some simple graded washes for depicting the volume of objects with shapes like a cylinder or globe. Draw a couple of cylinders and paint their sides with a light, clear water wash. Using a mixture of dark color like bluish gray, start applying paint vertically at one edge of the cylinder, move the wash almost to the center,

and then let the paint interact with the clear wash. To further vary the tone on this shaded side of the cylinder you can add additional color at the dark edge while the wash is still wet. This wash technique can be used to suggest the curved sides of other simple objects such as cups or bottles and is also helpful for sketching columns or tree trunks and branches. You can also use this wash technique for round objects such as balls. Sketch the outline of the shape, apply a clear wash, and begin adding color on the dark side of the object. To help control the degree of intermixing of colors, experiment with clear washes of different degrees of wetness. To help simulate the action of light on objects, add a shadow cast by the object.

DRY BRUSH

Dry brush watercolor techniques enable an extensive range of effects that can suggest textures of masonry and other rough materials or the play of light on different surfaces, such as water. For the example here, an old Spanish mission wall, washes were first used for general colors of the wall. Then an overall patina was applied to the wall by using a stiff brush to apply a light mixture of colors with light strokes in multiple directions (as shown upper right). Finally darker, more specific blotches were applied with a pointy brush by using a dabbing and dragging technique (shown middle right).

In the lakeshore example below, dry brush technique is combined with wet-in-wet washes to indicate ripples and splashes of the water. The blue of the lake is a reflection of the sky and, like the sky, it fades as it recedes into the distance. The whites are the sparkle due to the reflection of the sun.

Experiment with some of the effects shown here to get a feel for the possibilities of dry brushed watercolor.

GLAZING

In watercolor techniques, glazing refers to painting colors over other dried colors—sometimes in multiple layers. It is the basic approach to building watercolor sketches used in this book. Using glazing as a beginning technique affords better control over the process of painting. Practice this technique to better understand the process of building color and to explore a range of possibilities for color effects. For now, explore a few glazing combinations similar to the examples shown on the far right. Remember to always let the washes dry completely before adding a new wash. Use light strokes in multiple directions.

The example shown here is a segment from a larger painting of a barn in which several successive washes were added, beginning with the lightest and ending with the darkest. This is a good example of the transparency of shadows and shows that glazing need not always be simple uniform washes, but can have an interesting complexity.

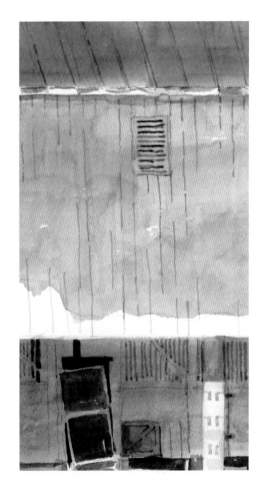

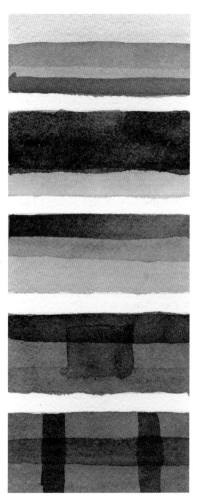

Step 1

BUILDING SKETCHES

Now that you are familiar with some of the basic techniques for applying watercolor, you can use them to build a watercolor sketch. For this exercise we begin with the building of a line drawing sketch in pencil to accommodate those with less experience in basic sketching or who are just coming back to sketching.

Sketch Exercise One

First, look at the photo carefully and identify some basic parts of the subject. Now draw a four-by-four-inch frame and place within it a few major organizing shapes, taking care to properly position them within the frame (step 1). Using these shapes as orienting devices, place other elements such

as the brushes and the outline of the small shell (step 2). Complete the basic sketch in pencil by adding some of the other features such as the edges of shadows and the ring marks on both the pitcher and the cup (step 3). Now you are ready to introduce color.

Step 2

Step 3

Step 4

Begin by applying a few large areas of color, taking care to avoid white spaces that you want to retain— reflections of light on the pitcher and the seashells, the rim of the cup and the brushes. You might start with the lightest color, the yellow, which provides the background; then add blue to the pitcher, the light gray to the cup, and the darker brown to the shell. Apply the colors as washes, taking care to keep the paint wet at the edges as you move from top to bottom. If you have excess water and color as you reach the end of the wash, wipe off the brush on a paper towel and use it to pick up the excess. For the purposes of this exercise you should focus more on the darkness of the colors than on depict- ing their exact hue (step 4). Once you are sure that the first coat of watercolor paint is completely dry, add graded washes to the pitcher, the cup, and the seashell. Apply a light coat of clear water over a figure such as the pitcher, and then starting at the darkest edge apply a mixture of dark color and continue toward the edge of the shadow, letting the

Step 5

Step 6

color mix with the clear water. You may need to pick up additional dark color to add to the dark edge but again let the colors mix by themselves as you did in the earlier exercise with washes. At this stage you may also apply medium-gray shadows to the small white seashell and the base of the brown shell and blue pitcher. Note also the small

shadows inside the cup (step 5). Finally, complete the sketch by indicating details such as the colors on the brush handles, the shadow of the tallest brush, and additional texture details of the white and brown seashells (step 6). Keep in mind that you're conveying your impression of the subject, not making an exact replica.

Don't become discouraged or self-critical if you don't get the same results as demonstrated here. Keep in mind this is the beginning of a learning process, not a contest. Relax and try to enjoy this exercise and the ones to follow. If you prefer, select subjects you find more interesting.

Sketch Exercise Two

Another subject might be as simple as a window. You could start with the example here or pick a window that is interesting to you. Beginning to notice your surroundings and identifying elements that are particularly appealing is part of the process of learning to sketch in watercolor. Developing your perceptive skills is an important element of sketching your environment.

Starting with a simple line drawing in pencil that establishes the basic elements of the subject, apply color to the frame of the window, which acts as an organizing element for the sketch and for the color range in which you work (step 1). Add shadow tones next to create the three-dimensionality of the window (step 2).

In the final sketch add detail elements and colors, including the objects on the windowsill, shadows in the windowpanes, and the dark areas of glass at the top (step 3). In this particular case we've proceeded from the middle tones of the window frame to the darker forms of the shadows to the high-contrast colors and values that provide the details. As you become more comfortable with sketching, you may want to move on to larger subjects such as the porch and entryway (page 28).

Step 1

Step 2

Step 3

Step 1

Sketch Exercise Three

When starting a sketch, it is important to identify the larger organizing shapes in the view—in this case the front entrance and side windows together with the large shadow cast by the porch overhang.

Begin painting by applying the large light color washes (step 1). Note that the color of the yellow wash of the doorway includes variations—a little more yellow in some areas and a little more pink in other areas. Color is rarely constant or uniform as we perceive it in real spaces.

Step 2

Step 3

Next apply the washes indicating shadows (step 2). Although the color of the shadow is quite dark it is important that it remain transparent so that we can see its impact on the door. If you're a little unsure about mixing color, try a sample of the door color on a scrap of watercolor paper and then paint some trial glazing washes to indicate the shadow color. You may notice that the shadows of the braces for the porch column are not exactly the same shape as the braces that cause them. Often in a sketch this is not important as long as the general effect is captured.

To complete the sketch, add details in the doorway and the porch column and railing construction (step 3).

Venice Afternoon by Thomas W. Schaller

2. ENVIRONMENT: SKETCH CONSTRUCTION

The history of our planet and the drama of human evolution are embedded in environments. Whether you're a professional designer or simply expanding your awareness of environments, there are endless opportunities for discovery. And whether you travel to other lands and cultures or explore your own hometown, sketching provides an effective and convenient means to absorb the richness of lessons that your surroundings may provide.

Now that the process of building a sketch is familiar, you're ready to tackle the more complex subject of environments. For convenience, we divide the subject of sketching environments into two chapters—one about sketch construction, the other concerned with tone and detail. In both chapters you undertake exercises that you can do at home or in a studio. At first you can sketch from pictures or slides, an accessible and convenient way to start your sketching practice. This is advantageous because it offers you access to a range of interesting subjects and views that have already been selected, cropped, and flattened into two-dimensional form. Not only are slides and photographs less intimidating than drawing directly from observing three-dimensional objects, but they also provide access to a greater variety of subjects than may be readily available nearby.

BUILDING THE SKETCH

In this exercise you can see a comparison of basic line sketching and watercolor sketching. This may be of particular use to those who have previous experience with line sketching and clarify for everyone the relative strengths of the two media. Try this example in both media. The processes for building a sketch and a watercolor are roughly parallel, but for watercolor it is best to always start the initial construction in light pencil.

Sketch Exercise Four

Within a frame of at least four-by-four inches, build the sketch with the largest shapes first and add only as much detail as necessary to position smaller elements such as windows and to indicate the edge of the shadow under the roof overhang (step 1).

The first application of color addresses the largest areas of light or middle tones in the sky, ground, and barn roof. Concentrate here on the proper balance of water and color and brush control. Keep in mind that wet applied color appears darker than when it has dried. Apply these washes with a half-inch flat wash brush for better control of the straight borders (step 2).

Add the darker tones of the shadows and land-

scape vegetation in the third step. To indicate the variation in tone and shapes of these natural items, use a round brush (step 3). Finish the sketch by adding a few details with a small, pointed brush. Avoid using a ready-made black pigment; create blacks from a combination of blue and brown pigments. A black hue that leans slightly toward blue helps to create a sense of depth or void for door and window openings (step 4).

Note that while the line drawing uses the simplest, most affordable tools, the watercolor sketch accomplishes multiple functions with rather simple means and includes many more dimensions of the experience of the subject.

Step 1

32

Step 2

Step 3

Step 4

33

Step 1

Step 2

Sketch Exercise Five

This is a grain elevator in southeastern Washington State. I picked it because it's an unusual subject that would not spring to mind when talking about fascinating views. I was drawn to the very subtle changes in the muted tones and the unusual effects created by a patchwork of repairs and torn pieces.

Again begin with a light pencil sketch to lay out the basic forms (step 1). Next lay down washes of the general color to unify the overall structure, and add a couple of minor objects to complete the composition (step 2). Then add a few elements of more intense color to provide some of the focal points of the sketch (step 3).

Now add volume-defining shadows to create a sense of depth (step 4). Finally, add a few typical elements such as the corrugated patterns on some of the materials and roof details to complete the sketch (step 5).

34

Step 3

Step 4

Step 5

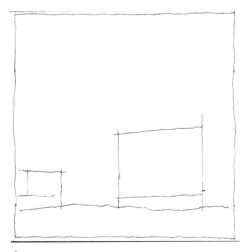

Step 1

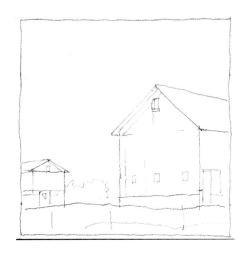

Step 2

Step 3

SKETCH-BUILDING EXAMPLES

Sketch Exercise Six

These pages illustrate the complete process of building a watercolor sketch, beginning with the very simple vertical and horizontal outlines that established the position of the major shapes of the barns (step 1). Once these are clearly in place, adding the other elements of the roofs and openings is relatively simple (step 2). The first watercolor washes establish the major background and foreground elements, the sky and the land (step 3). Next shade and shadows are added to define and illustrate the surfaces of both buildings (step 4). In the final frame several details are added—openings in the barns, textures of materials, small trees in the background, and a brief indication of the grasses and fence posts (step 5).

It is important to notice that the basic play of light on the structures is maintained throughout the whole process, capturing the feel of the space.

Step 4

Step 5

Mykonos, Greece (Photo by Vasily Makris)

Step 1

Step 2

Sketch Exercise Seven

Having outlined in pencil a subject you like (step 1), take time to identify the major features that attracted you before starting your sketch. Here it might be the intense glow of the Greek church complex caused by a setting sun in contrast with the cool blue of the sky and the deep rich colors of the foreground (steps 2–3). The vivid color of the buildings is further enhanced by the dark areas of shade and shadow (step 4). At the center of the sketch, note the subtle difference in the rendering of the adjacent shadows and shades (step 5).

Step 3

Step 4

Step 5

Step 1

Step 2

Sketch Exercise Eight

The key organizing element here is the diagonal slope of the hill. Once that profile is established by the sky and the sea, the basic composition of the sketch is set (step 1). The shade and shadows that define the forms and the play of light are kept rather simple, unifying the foreground (step 2). Darker washes define deeper shadows and graded washes help to define the cylindrical forms of the two towers, establishing them as points of interest (step 3). The details add expressive elements of the windmill and electric poles and lines (step 4). These final touches, together with the window and door openings, give a clear sense of scale to the subject.

Step 3

Step 4

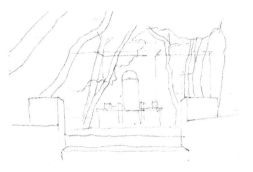

Step 1

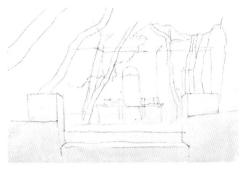

Step 2

Sketch Exercise Nine

This scene demonstrates the visual impact of multiple contrasts—light and dark, near and far, nature and built form, and high and low. The framing of the house facade by the opening through the cluster of dark trees provides the principal organization of the scene. This needs to be established in the initial pencil sketch (step 1) and reinforced as the layers of color are added (steps 2–3). Shades and shadows enhance the three-dimensional sense of the view (step 4). Because the first application of the dark colors of the trees in this demonstration tend to overwhelm the soft tones of the house, a color glazing is added to the house along with details in the final step. It is a good habit to check your results against your original intent before proceeding to each next step. Careful scrutiny of the subject and your sketch is as important as the process of applying color to your sketch.

Step 3

Step 4

42

Step 5

Sketch Exercise Ten

The old town of Bergamo, Italy, combines a labyrinth of medieval streets with civic buildings and piazzas of the Renaissance, producing a series of stimulating vistas. This opening to a narrow pedestrian street highlights the meeting of public and private space. The pencil drawing starts with the arched opening that serves as the organizing structure for the watercolor sketch (step 1). The approach to applying color varies from some of the previous sketches as the darkest tones are applied first (step 2). This establishes the range of values for the whole image. Subsequent steps add middle and lightest tones (step 3) with details indicated at the finish (step 4).

Step 1

44

Step 2

Step 3

Step 4

45

Sketch Exercise Eleven

Here is another experiment with a process of going from darkest to lightest tones. The value of the grass in the foreground was forced to provide a balance around the focal point of the sketch provided by the red barn. The darkest washes of the trees and the foreground grass set the upper end of the value range and reinforce the primacy of the central barn structure (step 1). Medium tones define the sky, landscape, and buildings (step 2). The lightest tones and dark shadows add depth to the scene (step 3). This balanced composition is energized by the definition of several smaller elements such as fences and the gas tank (step 4). Not much is seen of shade in this view but the shadows are important to defining the direction of the sun and the shape of the objects.

Step 1

Step 2

Step 3

Step 4

Step 1

Step 2

Sketch Exercise Twelve

The cylinder is the dominant form for the Guthrie Theatre by Jean Nouvel, making it a convenient starting point for a sketch (step 1). The effect of light falling on the cylinder is rendered by a wet-in-wet wash like that shown on page 19. You might want to practice the technique on a separate sheet before attempting it within this sketch. If you still have difficulty, try sketching at a smaller scale. The framing elements are the hill in the foreground and the rectangular forms to the left of the cylinder. All other forms hang on these foundations (step 2). Once more shade and shadow add further definition to the forms (step 3). Addition of a few hints of detail completes the image (step 4).

Step 3

Step 4

AFTER THE STORM · EVERGREEN, COLORADO

LEGGITT '98

Evergreen Sunset by Jim Leggitt, FAIA

3. ENVIRONMENT: TONE AND DETAIL

This chapter is intended to provide background to aid your understanding of the visual environment and sharpen your interest in visual acuity. Now that you have practiced the basics of building watercolor sketches, you can get the most out of the media of watercolor by closer consideration of tone and detail. Tone encompasses all the attributes of color including intensity, hue, and particularly value—the lightness or darkness of color. Detail encompasses those particulars that describe or identify the items in your sketches.

The use of tone plays a key role in defining the three-dimensionality of objects or environments because it can capture the form-defining characteristics of light. These include interaction with material shapes, colors, and textures, and the forming of shade, shadows, and reflections.

In this chapter, we first explore these dimensions of tone by representing them in watercolor. Then we consider the specific impacts of tone on capturing a view of an environment. Finally we deal with the role of detail and the methods for creating or capturing detail in watercolor. This includes looking at the overlap of tone and detail and how they can support each other to convey the important qualities and impacts of a specific environment.

TONE VALUES

Of the three qualities of color—hue, value, and intensity—value, the lightness or darkness of tone, may be the most influential in representing three-dimensional environments in watercolor. Whether in regard to objects or environments, light and atmosphere influence our perception of the visible world. Light—sunlight or artificial light—is important in defining the three-dimensionality of everything we see. Atmosphere acts as a filter for light as it travels from items in the environment to our eye. Whenever you are sketching, keep in mind the direction of light and its impacts on form as shade and shadow. Shade occurs on surfaces opposite to the direction of light or backside and is generally lighter than shadow due to the reflection of light from the sky. Shadows are caused by the blocking of light and appear on surfaces beyond the blocking object. One of the distinct advantages of watercolor is the ability to depict the transparency of shade and shadows.

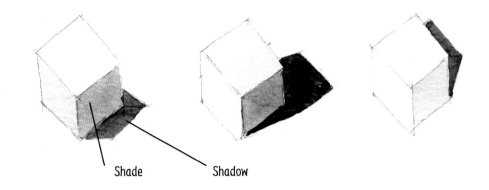

Shade   Shadow

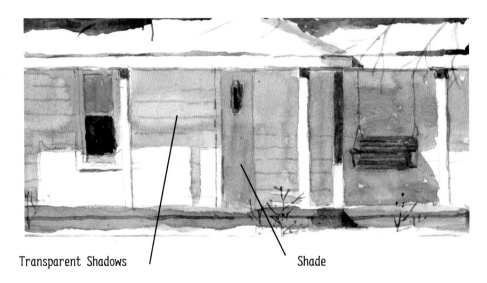

Transparent Shadows   Shade

Shade

Shadow

Atmosphere

Shadow

Shade

Shadow

Shade

Distance

53

ROLE OF COLOR VALUES

In preparation for integrating value with the other attributes of watercolor sketching, experiment with the full range of values for a color. The example here extends from light to dark grays, but also includes casts of warm and cool grays. Try reproducing the swatches at the bottom of these pages.

Notice that in this illustration the background sky and clouds are predominantly cool grays whereas the foreground colors of trees and buildings—even though very dark—have a warmer cast. The purpose here is to create a sense of depth by using cool hues that tend to recede in our perception and warmer hues that tend to move forward, closer to the viewer.

OBSERVING COLOR

To begin representing objects or environments in watercolor you must first realize that colors observed are rarely pure colors. More often they are mutations of pure color either by dilution or by graying. Observe the color samples shown here with the pure color from which they are derived indicated just below. Notice also that there are warm grays and cool grays.

Now we turn our attention to the skills of handling watercolor, starting with a review of the basics of color and the mixing of color. The top diagram shows the simplified relationships of color that many of us learned early in school, showing the effect of mixing the three basic colors blue, red, and yellow to produce secondary colors green, violet, and orange. Computer programs such as Photoshop can now produce idealized color combinations of this diagram, but for watercolor sketching we need to know more about the results of mixing actual pigments.

The second diagram uses the same color structure but with actual watercolor to show what happens when you begin to mix complementary colors such as red with green. The mixed colors appear on a line between the complementary pigments; each specific mixture has a larger proportion of the closest pigment.

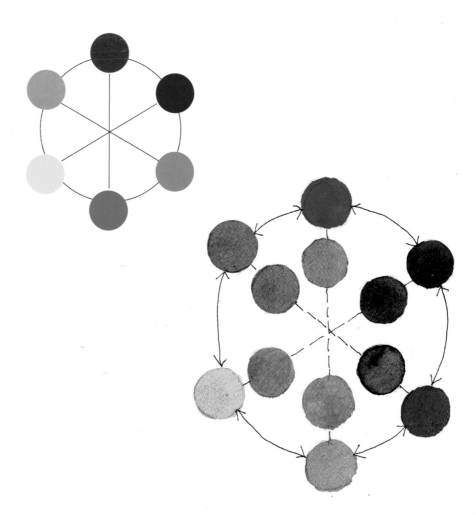

To get a better feel for mixing the range of color washes, paint swatches similar to those shown here. Start with a full-intensity color (upper left corner) and produce a range of increasingly lighter color (to the right) by gradually adding more water. Next add a small amount of a complementary color to the base color (here burnt umber was added to the cobalt blue), and then add water to create the range in the second row. Repeat the procedure for the third and fourth rows.

With this sense of control in hand, try loosening up by randomly experimenting with color variations as shown on the opposite page.

VALUE STUDIES

To heighten awareness of the role of values in your sketches, try doing a quick black-and-white study in which you try to distinguish the different levels of darkness of tones in the view. First, squint your eyes so as to blur the details, and then use a neutral color (either black or sepia) to lay down your darkest color. Next, add your medium grays and finally the lightest grays, leaving white as the brightest tone. This should help you in the future to size up the compositional effects of values.

The image opposite is rendered in what is called high-key color—mainly light and bright. The image above is one of low-key color—dark and intense. These represent two ends of the range of watercolor sketching challenges.

Here are a couple more challenging subjects to stretch your abilities. Again I recommend a black-and-white study as a guide to approaching the painting. Sketches like these might best be painted at nine-by-twelve-inch size or larger. For both examples a major feature—the skies—were rendered with loose wet-in-wet washes.

If at first these are overwhelming, try either doing a small segment of the image or doing it in a more abstract manner—not including as many details.

TONE AND DETAIL

In this example we begin to explore the overlap between tone and detail. The majority of the details in the porch sketch are caused by the play of light on the forms. Not all watercolor sketches need be of large-scale subjects such as landscapes or buildings. There is much to be learned in observation or sketching skills by concentrating on small subjects such as windows or doors.

Alfama

To conclude this series of examples challenge yourself by building a sketch of a subject that includes a range of shades and shadow plus interesting details. Working from a photo or slide, build your watercolor in a manner similar to that shown here. Note that details may be produced by small areas of color washes in addition to line work.

Castel Sant'Angelo by Jim Tice

4. SKETCHING IN THE FIELD

The expanding world of communication technology has provided unprecedented access to visual information. The combination of Internet, cell phone technology, and sophisticated search engines makes it possible to view images on any subject from anywhere. A wealth of information, visual and written, about Castel Sant'Angelo in Rome, for example, is instantly available. As useful as that can be, architects and designers know there's no substitute for the direct, on-site experience of visiting the Castel.

The full benefits of a watercolor sketching are realized in direct experiences of environments in the field. On-site, with all your senses engaged, sketching can provide a deeper understanding of those experiences. Consider the example of Castel Sant'Angelo. How is the experience influenced by the specific locations from where it is viewed? What variations in experience are derived from changes in weather or the time of day? How is the experience heightened by the contrasts between the Castel and the Tiber River?

You'll find sketching in the field an interesting and exhilarating experience. Often people will look over your shoulder in admiration or with a range of comments. With practice, you can be as unobtrusive or interactive with bystanders as you wish. The previous chapters were devoted to developing your watercolor sketching skills, interest, and confidence to support the ultimate goal of being able to sketch what you want, where you want, and when you want. This chapter provides a practical guide to sketching in a variety of circumstances in the field.

EQUIPMENT

The end goal is to develop proficiency and confidence in watercolor sketching. The best route to achieving this is developing the habit of sketching. Choose equipment that is appropriate to your skill level and provides you with the ease to sketch anywhere and anytime. The equipment choices shown here are organized into three categories based on level of experience, quality of materials, and choice of subject.

Basic/Journal

These are the basic items you'll need to get into the habit of sketching:

- small watercolor sketchpad or watercolor block (five-by-seven-inch or seven-by-ten-inch) that is easy to carry and can be kept at hand most of the time

- basic set of brushes (half-inch wash, no.6 or no. 8 round, and a no. 1 round)

- compact travel palette with a set of pan colors and mixing area

- small cup or jar for water

- paper towels

Try to find watercolor pads with as many pages as possible and that can accept watercolor on both sides of each page. Use good synthetic brushes that retain their shape and good quality watercolors.

Intermediate Level

These items are appropriate for the more advanced sketcher and more extensive travel:

- watercolor block (nine-by-twelve-inch or twelve-by-sixteen-inch)

- brushes (a couple of flat wash ranging from half inch to an inch, a no. 8 or no. 10 round, a no. 1 or no. 2 round, and a small rigger brush for fine lines)

- larger airtight travel palette that can accommodate watercolor paint from tubes

- watertight plastic jar

- several shop towels (durable heavy-duty disposable towels found in hardware stores)

- shoulder bag to carry all your equipment, plus a small camera, cell phone or other communication devices

SELECTING AND FRAMING THE VIEW

Effective field sketches begin with moving about the site to find the most interesting view. This is followed by a brief study of how to frame the view— deciding what to include in the sketch and choosing a vertical or horizontal orientation. I opted at the sketch stage to omit the larger tree to the right of the house. The pencil sketch started the watercolor process.

The building of the watercolor sketch then pro-
ceeds in the usual sequence: major area washes,
secondary areas, shade and shadow, and final
details.

OBSERVATION

Watercolor sketching can act as a important research tool for understanding how environments affect people. In the sketch above you can see how natural light helps define shapes and creates points of interest to catch the eye. The effect of the sketch is to capture just the major elements of forms in space and the mood that the early morning light creates.

A smaller sketch to the right focuses on the detail of the window and the flowers in a more intimate setting. Here it is important to render the relative values in a low-key shade-dominant view.

Every now and then you encounter something unusual or unique that was unexpected, such as the goat in this painting and what looks like a rather rundown building. The building had an eerie, almost sinister feeling too tempting to pass up.

Don't be afraid to jump in and try to capture what you can; doing so challenges you to stretch your abilities.

Wherever you are, seek out a variety of views at different scales. Use watercolor sketching as a way to expand your perception of environment. The view of Santorini, in Greece, above, contrasts the rich colors of the foreground vegetation with the serene muted tones of the far-off hills and sea.

Seek new or unfamiliar subjects and be open to new experiences and perceptions. You never know what will catch your eye and introduce a new level of awareness. Pick out some subjects of more limited scope where you can concentrate and not worry about rushing yourself. The sketches shown here are simple, showing just a few basic forms. Remember: the experience of sketching in watercolor should be one you enjoy. Always take enough time to relax and focus.

Subjects on coastal waters are a great source of contrasts between nature and the man-made environment. Among some of the features are the vast contrast in scale and the constantly changing weather patterns. Even the air and sounds can provide inspiration that is invigorating and enjoyable.

TIME LIMITS

While sketching on-site you may occasionally lack the time to complete a normal watercolor. One option is to include the unique elements of the subject and note only a sample of the redundant elements such as windows or wall treatment. This allows you to finish the sketch off-site. In this example the brick and stone patterns are repetitive. Only enough of one of the windows is completed to guide finishing the other windows. But specifics of this scene such as the edges of shadows or the cluster of flowers are recorded.

Another approach would eliminate details, focusing on a simple rendition of the composition as in the example above. Or the palette of colors can be greatly constrained as in the Greek church sketch at the left.

PEOPLE

As you progress with sketching, include people in your sketches. This gives a sense of scale to the view and some sense of the activity or use of the space. In the sketch shown you can see that it does not take much indication of detail to give some sense of the crowd and of a few individuals closer to you. The illustration at the top of the opposite page shows several people walking on the same level at various distances from the sketcher. Note that in most cases no matter how distant, their heads are approximately on the same level. These figures were created with fairly simple blocks of color to give some indication of the head or hair and legs.

As you get involved to a greater degree with watercolor sketching you may want to include figures at a larger scale, closer at hand and with more detail. As before, the simplest approach is to start with a rough pencil sketch and then add watercolor. Just as with sketching environments be aware of the direction of light as it illuminates human figures. Try to capture the role of people in the space by their activity or interaction with each other. This is another way to note the impact of environments on people.

TREES

Trees are generally represented as skeletons of limbs, as masses of leaves, or a combination of both—depending on the season of the year and distance from the sketcher. With sketching experience you'll notice the characteristic limb patterns and overall shapes of different tree species. It is important to represent the volume and shape of trees by recognizing the direction of the source of light. From a distance tree shapes may be quite simple, but more variations or subshapes are apparent when viewed closer.

SKETCHBOOK/JOURNAL

Keeping a small sketchbook for line drawings and notes can be a helpful complement to watercolor sketching. In addition to building observation and sketching skills, a sketchbook provides a convenient place for notes and reflections on your experiences. (For additional background in basic line media, see the companion book, *Freehand Sketching*.)

Summer Palace

Hydra 6/92

Michele
P. Jones

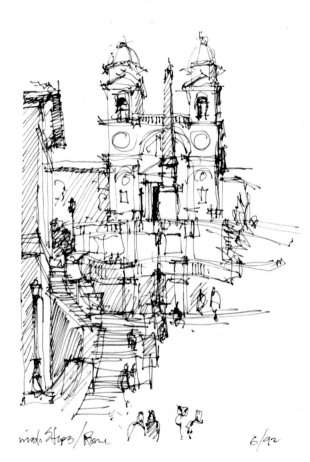

inside Steps / Rome

6/92

91

Taking a Moment—Watercolor and digital rendering

5. WATERCOLOR IN THE STUDIO

Thus far we've focused on the processes of creating watercolor sketches; in this chapter we deal primarily with sharing watercolor sketches with others. We consider the benefits of editing, expanding, altering, and sharing the content of watercolor sketches. While sketching can be an important tool for individual growth, there is potential for even more impact of sketches in the processes of communicating with others.

A studio or other location can provide space, time, and support for creative development and extension of sketching. A few devices—digital camera, scanner, computer, Internet—open a wide range of communication possibilities. You can pursue designs or other creative projects at your preferred pace. The studio is a place to both be alone with your thoughts and connected to a broad collection of people and ideas as you choose.

This chapter provides a limited set of examples, offered as a hint to extend the possibilities of watercolor sketching, and to encourage you to explore other applications.

REPAINTING

Watercolor sketching on-site has many benefits. Often there is a special intensity or excitement that is communicated in the finished work that is hard to duplicate when working from a photo or in a studio. But sometimes you might want to further explore a sketch subject via a larger sketch or painting. In such cases, a controlled environment such as a studio allows you a more leisurely but intense study. For this example, a photo of the original small sketch (above) was converted to black and white and cropped in Photoshop to restudy the composition of the subject. With the use of a grid overlay (in red) a pencil sketch was created at a larger scale, allowing for more detail in the final watercolor.

DIGITAL SUBJECTS

In another application of computer resources, a filter was applied to the original photo (above, left), somewhat abstracting the shapes. Cropping was then applied to create the composition of the subject for the final sketch.

The final watercolor sketch (opposite) is quite loose and more inspired by the view than any attempt to record details. The focus is on the contrast of the white-clad figure and the lush colorful forms of the landscape. You might want to try this approach after you have enough experience to feel comfortable with the media. Remember to explore watercolor and avoid being overly self-critical.

EXPERIMENTS IN STYLES

Sometimes it's beneficial to emulate different styles to stretch your experience with watercolor. Here are four different interpretations of a windmill. They each represent one person's perception of what is interesting about the windmill. There's a good chance that none of them exactly replicates the actual building as captured by a camera.

Pick out one or two images and see if you can repeat them. It is not important that you make an exact copy; the value is more in the process and helping you to look and commit watercolor to paper. Have fun with this exercise. You might try a version of your own unlike any of these.

99

MIXED MEDIA

The studio can also provide the opportunity to
experiment with mixed media. For these examples
photographs from a trip to Portugal provided the
sketch subjects. In each case a line sketch was
made with a fine-line, waterproof marker on hot-
press watercolor paper. Watercolor washes were
then added to capture the color and play of light.
The less rushed environment of the studio allowed
for more expression of detail than might otherwise
have been included.

DIGITAL VALUE STUDIES

You're already familiar with the utility of mono-
tone value studies in preparing for a watercolor
sketch. Digital graphic editing programs such as
Photoshop provide another means to make value
studies of a subject. To simplify shapes a filter is
applied to the original photo, and then desaturated
to concentrate attention on the pattern of different
value tones.

DIGITAL EDITING

Modifications of this sketch of Mykonos, Greece, were made by digitally altering a specific color without changing or diminishing the tactile quality of hand-applied watercolor.

On the opposite page the image of the Greek church shows digital filtering applied to a sketch to simplify and intensify graphic impact.

At right, alterations of color and contrast were made to the entire image of St. Paul's Cathedral, London.

STUDIO PROJECT

The illustration opposite was developed using several photographs as resource material. Because there were several requirements for what the image must include, several sketch studies were needed for development of the final content and arrangement. Two of these studies are shown below. On the left is an early line drawing of the principal forms and composition. On the right is a later study elaborating on the image content by using mixed media of line drawing, digitally rendered tones, and colored pencil. The studio provided the proper environment and tools for both the development studies and the final rendering of the illustration.

CONCLUSION

Throughout this book, I have introduced you to the benefits of adopting the habit and skills of watercolor sketching. My hope is that you're encouraged, as I once was, to discover the potential and rewards of watercolor. This medium can be an immensely rewarding pursuit, an enriching view not only of the world and people around you, but also an insight into your own perceptions of that world. Exploring the study of design, and architectural design in particular, through this medium hones your skills in visual acuity and perception, increases your facility and fluidity in the design process, and provides a means to personal satisfaction.

Watercolor sketching can also be simply a source of delight, a process in which you can become completely absorbed. It can be an enjoyable physical experience—the feel of the paper and the movement of your brush across the surface become part of the stimulation and reward of sketching. Accomplished sketchers know that the quality of their images ultimately derives from these experiences of awareness, concentration, and touch. If you fully engage in the process you'll have moments of pure delight such as I had on an encounter with itinerant street musicians in Paris. The image I captured speaks more to me than a photograph ever could.

ILLUSTRATION CREDITS

RECOMMENDED READING

Ching, Francis D. K. *Drawing: A Creative Process*. New York, 1989.
———. *Sketches from Japan*. New York, 2000.
Cooper, Douglas. *Drawing and Perceiving*, 3rd ed. New York, 2000.
Crawshaw, Alwyn. *The Half-Hour Painter*. Cincinnati, 1990.
Crowe, Norman, and Paul Laseau. *Visual Notes for Architects and Designers*, 2nd ed. New York, 2012.

Hogarth, Paul. *Drawing Architecture: A Creative Approach*. New York, 1973.
———. *Drawing People*. New York, 1971.
Kautzky, Ted. *The Ted Kautzky Pencil Book*, comb. ed. New York, 1979.
Laseau, Paul. *Freehand Sketching*. New York, 2004.
Nicolaides, K. *The Natural Way to Draw*. Boston, 1975.

Reid, Charles. *Charles Reid's Watercolor Secrets*. Cincinnati, 2004.
Scarry, Huck. *Venice Sketchbook*. New York, 1994.
Stabin, Mel. *Watercolor: Simple, Fast, and Focused*. New York, 1999.
White, Edward T. *Path, Portal, Place: Appreciating Public Space in Urban Environments*. Tallahassee, 1999.

INDEX